A STEP INTO HISTORY™

IMMIGRATION & AMERICA

BY STEVEN OTFINOSKI

Series Editor

Elliott Rebhun, Editor & Publisher,

The New York Times Upfront

at Scholastic

SCHOLASTIC

Content Consultant: James Marten, PhD, Professor and Chair,
History Department, Marquette University, Milwaukee, Wisconsin

Cover: An Italian immigrant woman and her children at Ellis Island in 1908

Library of Congress Cataloging-in-Publication Data
Names: Otfinoski, Steven, author.
Title: Immigration & America / by Steven Otfinoski.Other titles: Immigration
    and America
Description: New York, NY : Children's Press, [2018] | Series: A step into
    history | Includes bibliographical references and index.
Identifiers: LCCN 2017030751| ISBN 9780531226896 (library binding) | ISBN
    9780531230114 (pbk.)
Subjects: LCSH: United States—Emigration and immigration—History—
    Juvenile literature. | Immigrants—United States—History—Juvenile
    literature.
Classification: LCC JV6450 .O4 2018 | DDC 304.8/73009—dc23 LC record
    available at https://lccn.loc.gov/2017030751

Scholastic Inc., 557 Broadway, New York, NY 10012.

1 2 3 4 5 6 7 8 9 10 R 27 26 25 24 23 22 21 20 19 18

CONTENTS

PROLOGUE

You will find the definitions of bold words in the glossary on pages 140-41.

FROM ITS VERY BEGINNING, AMERICA HAS been a land of immigrants. Its people have brought energy and ideas from all over the world. While people came to America as immigrants, they and their descendants gradually **assimilated** into the American way of life and became proud Americans themselves.

What draws people to America, from the first people to arrive thousands of years ago to today's most recent immigrants? The question has perhaps as many answers as there are immigrants. Everyone has their own reasons for wanting to start a new life in a new country. Since its birth as a nation, the United States has offered a shining promise of freedom, **democracy**, and opportunity. It was irresistible to the earliest immigrants from Europe. Some lived in countries that had been ruled by all-powerful monarchs and noblemen for hundreds or even thousands of years. They worked the land of rich people while seeing little change in their own fortunes from one generation to the next. Others came from countries that were democratic, but poor. Some were starving in their home countries. Many were discriminated against or even attacked for their religious beliefs. America offered all of these immigrants a new beginning. Moving to the United States gave people a chance to own land, start a business, escape oppression, and pursue their dreams for themselves and their children. These dreams are still alive in the hearts of today's immigrants.

Since the colonial era, many Americans have sought to slow down or even halt immigration. Does there come a point when immigration is no longer positive for the United States? Do national security and economic concerns outweigh the benefits of immigration? These questions are very much on the minds of many Americans today. The answers and solutions may lie, as they often do, in the past. By looking deeper into the history of immigration in the United States, we will be able to better understand its importance in today's complex and challenging world.

Early Native American people shaped arrowheads and spearheads from stone and used them to hunt a variety of animals.

CHAPTER 1

THE FIRST IMMIGRANTS

The first Americans were also the first immigrants.

FOR MILLIONS OF YEARS, THERE WERE NO people in the Americas. Then, about a million years ago, during the last Ice Age, all of North America was covered in ice. As a result, the oceans sank lower and land that was once underwater rose above the ocean's surface. A land bridge emerged between Siberia in Asia and Alaska in North America.

About 15,000 years ago, people began crossing over this land bridge to the Americas. Less than 7,000 years later, these peoples had settled from Alaska to the tip of South America. At first, these early Native Americans were nomadic hunters and gatherers. Over time, many of them settled in more permanent communities and grew crops to eat. In each region, people developed their own languages and cultures.

For several thousand years, Native Americans had North America to themselves. When the first European explorers arrived in America by accident at the end of the 15th century, there were millions of Native Americans in the present-day United States.

Thinking he had reached the East Indies in Asia, explorer Christopher Columbus mistakenly called the native people he met in America "Indians."

Huge, elephant-like animals called mammoths were once an important source of food for the people of North America.

The Pilgrims were a group of English immigrants who sailed across the Atlantic Ocean to America aboard a ship called the Mayflower in 1620.

CHAPTER 2

THE ENGLISH ARRIVE

Some came for religious freedom.
Others came for land or to get rich.

AFTER CHRISTOPHER COLUMBUS BROUGHT news of the Americas back to Europe, explorers from Spain, Portugal, and other European countries soon began their own journeys across the Atlantic. The English were among the Europeans to send settlers to the present-day United States to start colonies. They founded Jamestown in what is now Virginia in 1607. It was the first permanent English settlement in North America. Some English immigrants were middle-class people and noblemen who came in search of wealth. Many grew prosperous growing tobacco.

However, at first, most English immigrants came to Virginia as **indentured servants**. They were poor people whose passage to America was paid by established settlers. After arriving, the servants worked for these settlers for a period of time to pay off their passage. At the end of that time, they were free to start their own lives in America.

By 1732, there were 13 English colonies in America. By the end of the century, the colonies would become the United States of America.

In the colonial era (1607–1775), an estimated one million immigrants came to America from Europe.

English settlers walk through snow on their way to church. A lack of food and shelter made winters especially difficult for early English settlers.

The Dutch East India Company was a Dutch company that shipped goods to and from countries all around the world. It was so wealthy and powerful that it minted its own coins.

CHAPTER 3

THE DUTCH AND THE FRENCH

Dutch and French settlers were better
at trading than building colonies.

I N 1609, EXPLORER HENRY HUDSON SAILED up the Hudson River and claimed the land along its banks for the Dutch. This was the beginning of New Netherlands, the largest Dutch settlement in America. Because of its location and excellent port, it became an important trading center. In 1664, the English seized New Amsterdam, the largest city in New Netherlands, and renamed it New York. Many of the Dutch settlers stayed.

Around the same time, the French established the colony of New France in what is now Canada. By the early 1700s, England and France were engaged in a struggle for control of North America. The English emerged the victors in 1763, after the French and Indian War. However, France still controlled the vast Mississippi River valley. The English colonists declared their independence in 1776 and established the United States. In 1803, President Thomas Jefferson purchased the Mississippi River valley region from France. This transaction came to be called the Louisiana Purchase. French influence and culture are still strong today in the state of <u>Louisiana</u> and in northern New England, where many French Canadians settled.

Louisiana is one of several states with French names. Others include Maine and Vermont.

A Dutch ship arrives in New Amsterdam. New Amsterdam, located on the tip of Manhattan Island, had a busy port.

The Millheim Journal *was a Pennsylvania newspaper that published articles in both English and German in the 1800s and 1900s.*

CHAPTER 4

GERMAN IMMIGRANTS

Arriving in America soon after the
English, German immigrants assimilated
well in their new homeland.

SEVEN MILLION GERMANS HAVE IMMIGRATED to the United States since 1776. However, Germany never established colonies in America. This was largely because Germany was for centuries a collection of small kingdoms that weren't unified as one nation. Political problems at home were one reason Germans came to America. Others were religious persecution, unfair taxes, and war. Most of the first German arrivals, from about 1640 to the early 1800s, settled in New York and Pennsylvania.

The English looked down on these early German immigrants as uneducated and poor. Even Benjamin Franklin spoke out against German immigrants. After the German Revolution of 1848, well-educated, middle-class Germans came to America in large numbers. They formed their own communities and kept their own language, but were largely respected. As they assimilated into American life, Germans became more accepted as Americans and not just immigrants.

"Why should Pennsylvania, founded by the English, become a colony of aliens, who shortly will be so numerous as to Germanize us instead of us Anglicizing them?" Franklin wrote in 1751.

Many German families, such as the one pictured here, eventually settled in Kansas, where they became farmers.

66 *The tract through which we passed is generally very good land, with plenty of water.* **99**

—Father Junípero Serra, writing of
San Diego in a letter to a friend

CHAPTER 5

SPANISH SETTLERS IN CALIFORNIA

With a string of 21 **missions**, the Spanish left an impressive legacy in California.

Find out more about people whose names appear in orange and bold on pages 134–35.

THE SPANISH BEGAN SETTLING IN THE Americas in the early 1500s. By 1542, Spain had built a colonial empire centered on gold and land in the West Indies, Mexico, and Peru. By the late 1600s, the Spanish had moved north into present-day New Mexico, Arizona, and California, which were all then part of Mexico.

In 1769 a priest named **Father Junípero Serra** founded the first Catholic mission near what is now San Diego, California. Over the next 50 years, the Spanish established 21 missions along the California coast. There, they converted Native Americans to Christianity and taught them skills such as farming and weaving. However, the priests often treated the native peoples poorly. By 1846, the missions were closed by the Mexican government, which had won independence from Spain. California would soon break with Mexico, briefly be an independent republic, and then join the United States in 1848.

Father Serra and his followers built the missions just far enough apart that each was one day's journey from the next by foot.

Father Junípero Serra (left) watches as missionaries install a cross to found Mission San Diego. This mission later became the site of San Diego, California.

A boat carrying America's
first 20 African slaves
arrives in Virginia.

OCT NOV DEC **1619** JAN FEB MAR

CHAPTER 6

UNWILLING IMMIGRANTS: AFRICAN SLAVES

They were among the first immigrants in colonial America, but they came against their will.

By 1860, shortly before the start of the Civil War, there were 4.5 million African Americans. Only about 500,000 of them were free.

I N 1619, A DUTCH SHIP ARRIVED IN JAMESTOWN carrying 20 Africans. This marked the beginning of slavery in the American colonies. In the following years, countless people were captured in Africa and shipped across the Atlantic Ocean to be sold as slaves in America.

By 1790, there were <u>750,000 enslaved Africans</u> in America. Like other immigrants, Africans brought along their traditions, languages, and music. They found in them a source of comfort amid the cruelties of slavery. Slaves served their owners for life and had no rights. Their children were slaves as well. Most worked in tobacco, rice, and cotton fields, while a small number worked as house servants and cooks. They often suffered physical abuse from their masters and had very poor living conditions.

Slavery officially ended after the Civil War (1861–1865). Today, most African Americans are descendents of slaves.

This slave family lived in Savannah, Georgia, in the 1860s. After the Civil War, large numbers of former slaves moved from the South to other parts of the country.

The U.S. Constitution, which was adopted in 1787, outlines the structure of the U.S. government but has little to say about the country's immigration process.

CHAPTER 7

MORE IMMIGRANTS TO A NEW NATION

The new United States of America needed

immigrants to become a strong nation.

INCREASING TAXATION AND A LACK OF representation in the British government led the colonies to revolt in 1775. The Revolution ended in 1783 with the 13 colonies defeating Britain and establishing an independent nation. The U.S. Constitution, adopted in 1787, does not provide guidelines for how newcomers could become American citizens. All it says is that "All persons born or **naturalized** in the United States, and subject to the jurisdiction thereof, are citizens of the United States and of the State wherein they reside." It also gives Congress the power to establish rules for naturalization.

The Naturalization Act was passed by Congress in 1790 to accommodate the country's growing number of immigrants. It said that any "free white person" of good character could apply for citizenship after living in the country for two years. Once approved for citizenship, the person had to take the Oath of Allegiance to the Constitution. While the law opened the doors for citizenship for many, it left out indentured servants and slaves.

After leading the American forces to victory in the Revolutionary War, George Washington (center) was elected to be the first President of the United States.

The color green and the "Maid of Erin" flag are symbols of Irish pride.

CHAPTER 8

FLEEING IRELAND'S FAMINE

The Irish had been coming to America for years,
but a natural disaster in the 1840s led them to
flee their home country in large numbers.

The potato famine was not confined to Ireland. Other European countries, including Germany, experienced it, too.

I RISH IMMIGRANTS WERE AMONG THE EARLIEST to come to America. They even introduced the white potato to America in 1719. Potatoes were a staple food of millions of poor farm families in Ireland. So when **blight** killed off the potato crop in 1845, it led to <u>widespread famine.</u> Over a two-year period, 750,000 Irish died of starvation or disease. Hundreds of thousands more **emigrated** to America to begin new lives.

By 1860, there were 1.5 million Irish in America, making them the largest immigrant group of the time. Most of these newcomers were poor and uneducated and could not compete with other Americans for jobs. Most of the men became laborers, and most of the women worked as servants or washed clothes. Over time, their children and grandchildren rose up the social ladder.

Irish Americans are a vibrant part of America today, but they have lost none of their love for their homeland. During St. Patrick's Day parades in many American towns and cities, they proudly proclaim their motto in the old Gaelic language, *"Erin go bragh."* It means "Ireland forever."

A ship full of Irish immigrants leaves Ireland for America in 1903.

A Know-Nothing flag displays an anti-immigrant message.

CHAPTER 9

THE KNOW-NOTHING PARTY

Growing anti-immigrant feelings in the 1840s
gave birth to a new political party.

BY THE 1840S, SOME AMERICANS WERE becoming disturbed by the increasing flow of immigrants, especially from Ireland and Germany. These Americans, mostly Protestants, looked down on the largely Roman Catholic immigrants as poor and inferior. They also feared they might lose their jobs to the newcomers.

In 1849, opponents of immigration formed a secret society called the Order of the Star-Spangled Banner. By 1854, there were enough of them across the country to form a national political organization, the American Party, which became known as the Know-Nothing Party.

Two years later, the Know-Nothings launched a presidential campaign. Their platform called for strict limits on immigration and regulations that would make it harder for immigrants to become citizens. The party nominated former U.S. president **Millard Fillmore** as their presidential candidate. Fillmore won a surprising 21 percent of the vote, but he only won one state, Maryland. The Know-Nothings soon disappeared, but the anti-immigrant feelings they tapped into did not.

When asked about their secret activities, party members said they "knew nothing."

This sheet music for an anti-immigrant song proclaims a character called Citizen Know-Nothing to be Uncle Sam's Youngest Son. Uncle Sam is a popular symbol of patriotic feelings.

UNCLE SAM'S YOUNGEST SON

CITIZEN

KNOW NOTHING.

A total of about $2 billion worth of gold was mined in California during the gold rush.

CHAPTER 10

CHINATOWNS ACROSS AMERICA

They came for gold and stayed to find a
better life, but they also faced prejudice.

THE DISCOVERY OF GOLD IN CALIFORNIA
in 1848 brought thousands of people to
America's West Coast in hopes of striking it
rich. Among them were Chinese immigrants
who wanted to escape economic hardship after Great
Britain defeated China in the first Opium War (1839–
1842). Few Chinese got rich during the gold rush,
but they did find new opportunities in San Francisco.
Some opened restaurants, introducing Californians
to Chinese food. Others went to work building a
transcontinental railroad connecting California to the
East Coast. Many Americans found Chinese customs
strange. They forced the new immigrants to live in
neighborhoods called Chinatowns.

Most Chinese immigrants were hard workers,
which may have been another reason they faced so
much discrimination. Californians didn't like the
competition for jobs, especially when the Chinese were
willing to work for lower wages. In 1882, with about
115,000 Chinese immigrants living in the United
States, Congress passed the Chinese Exclusion Act,
banning all Chinese immigration for 10 years. The act
was renewed several times. No Chinese immigrants
were allowed into the United States again until 1943.

Japanese immigrants, initially
welcomed through a trade
treaty, were also restricted
by the early 1900s.

*Chinese immigrants carry a basket
full of gifts to celebrate Chinese
New Year in San Francisco's
Chinatown in the early 1900s.*

Utah's Golden Spike National Historic Site marks the location where the transcontinental railroad was completed in 1869.

CHAPTER 11

WORKING ON THE RAILROAD

The race to complete the first transcontinental
railroad pitted two immigrant groups against
each other, but for a good cause.

THE FIRST RAILROAD TO CROSS THE UNITED States was built with the strength and courage of Chinese and Irish laborers. The 1,775-mile (2,857-kilometer) transcontinental route stretched from Omaha, Nebraska, where the railroad ended at the time, to Sacramento, California. A company called the Central Pacific Railroad worked eastward from Sacramento, employing mostly Chinese workers. The Union Pacific moved westward from Omaha, employing mainly Irish people.

The Chinese workers had the more challenging route. They had to blast rock through the Sierra Nevada mountains and dig it out to make tunnels for trains. Many of them lost their lives in ill-timed explosions or fell to their deaths from the mountainsides. The Irish workers faced serious obstacles, too. While the Great Plains region was flat, which made it easier to lay down tracks, the workers had to contend with heavy storms and attacks from Native Americans. In the end, the two railroads met up at Promontory Point in Utah, on May 10, 1869. It was a great moment for America and for the proud immigrants who built the transcontinental railroad.

Chinese laborers work on the transcontinental railroad in Nevada.

Advertisements made the journey to America seem fun and exciting.

CHAPTER 12

THE GREAT IMMIGRATION (1880-1920)

They came from more than a dozen countries, a stream of humanity that didn't cease for 40 years.

UNTIL THE 1870S, THE VAST MAJORITY of immigrants to America came from northern and western Europe. But from 1880 to 1920, a great flood of immigrants started coming from southern Europe, eastern Europe, Russia, and Scandinavia. This wave of new Americans was known as the Great Immigration.

The Scandinavians headed for the Great Plains, where they became farmers. They were lured by emigrant agents in Europe who were hired by U.S. state governments, especially in the Midwest and West, where more people were needed to clear the land and pay taxes. Emigrant agents greatly exaggerated the American landscape with misleading pictures, pamphlets, and talk. In return, they were paid a fee for each person they convinced to emigrate.

Others heard how great America was in letters from friends who had already moved there. Many immigrants believed the hype and expected to find the streets of America paved with gold. Disillusioned, some returned home quickly. But many more stayed to find a new and better life in America.

A Scandinavian family in Wisconsin in the late 1800s shows off their four spinning wheels, which are used to turn materials such as cotton or wool into yarn.

During the Great Immigration, signs written in Hebrew were a common sight in New York City's Jewish neighborhoods.

CHAPTER 13

JEWISH IMMIGRANTS

Driven out of Europe by prejudice and religious persecution, Jewish immigrants took full advantage of opportunities in their new homeland.

EWISH IMMIGRANTS WERE AN EARLY presence in America. The first Jews in North America arrived in New Amsterdam in 1654. By 1776, the year the colonies declared their independence from Great Britain, there were 2,500 practicing Jews in America. About 200,000 German Jews arrived in the United States between 1840 and 1860. They were well-educated, middle-class people who brought useful skills to the growing nation.

The three million Jews who came to America during the Great Immigration were not as fortunate. Many of these immigrants were fleeing **pogroms** in eastern and central Europe and Russia, the result of prejudice and religious intolerance. These people were poor and uneducated, but also hardworking and deeply religious. Many of them settled in cities in the Northeast. In New York City, they lived on the Lower East Side of Manhattan in densely packed neighborhoods. They found jobs as factory workers, especially in the garment industry, and pushcart peddlers, selling everything from used clothing to fruits and vegetables.

At markets like this one in New York City, Jewish pushcart peddlers sold a wide variety of products to their fellow immigrants.

Ships regularly traveled between the United States and Europe carrying mail, goods, and new immigrants.

CHAPTER 14

ROUGH CROSSING IN STEERAGE

Reaching the United States was a daunting challenge for millions of immigrants.

Often a father would make the voyage alone, find work in America, and then send money home for the rest of the family to join him.

IN THE DAYS BEFORE AIR TRAVEL, <u>EUROPEAN immigrants came to America by boat</u> across the Atlantic Ocean. At first, they came on sailing ships that took five to six weeks to make the crossing. Unable to pay for regular passenger cabins, most immigrants traveled the cheapest way, in **steerage**. This space below deck was originally meant to hold freight and livestock.

The immigrants were packed tightly in steerage, which had little or no light and no ventilation. They slept in narrow bunk beds stacked three high. These crowded quarters allowed disease to spread with frightening speed, and many immigrants died of illness and were buried at sea. Other risks came from powerful storms that sank many ships.

By the start of the Great Immigration in the late 1800s, sailing ships had been replaced by steamships. This reduced the voyage to 14 days. However, in the terrible conditions of steerage—which didn't change on these new ships—even two weeks felt like a lifetime of misery.

Steerage passengers enjoy a rare breath of fresh air above deck aboard a ship in 1899.

A plaque bearing Emma Lazarus's poem "The New Colossus" has hung inside the Statue of Liberty since 1903.

CHAPTER 15

LADY LIBERTY

A symbol of American freedom and hospitality, the Statue of Liberty was a gift from the people of France.

NEW YORK WAS BY FAR THE BIGGEST POINT of entry for immigrants to the United States. After the long and arduous journey across the Atlantic, one of the first things immigrants saw as they sailed into New York Harbor was the Statue of Liberty. "The bigness of Mrs. Liberty overcomes us . . . she was like a goddess," recalled one Polish immigrant. This goddess was the brainchild of French sculptor **Frederic Auguste Bartholdi**, who wanted to honor America's spirit of freedom, which was admired around the world. The 151-foot (46-meter) statue took about 10 years to build, with dozens of workers laboring in France under Bartholdi's direction. When finished, it was disassembled and shipped to New York in 214 packing crates. The statue was reassembled on Bedloe's Island— renamed Liberty Island—and dedicated on October 28, 1886, by President Grover Cleveland.

Inside the statue's pedestal is engraved the famous sonnet "The New Colossus" by poet <u>Emma Lazarus</u>. The poem encourages other nations to send their forgotten and needy people to America.

Lazarus worked tirelessly to organize aid for persecuted Jews coming to the United States.

The highest point of the Statue of Liberty's torch reaches 305.5 feet (93 m) above the ground.

*Some 12 million immigrants
passed through Ellis Island
on their way to new lives
in the United States.*

CHAPTER 16

ELLIS ISLAND

It was the first stop in this new land for millions of immigrants, but for some it was their last stop in America.

FROM 1892 TO 1943, THE FIRST DESTINATION for immigrants coming into New York was Ellis Island. Visiting the island was an experience that few would ever forget. In a great hall with a maze of lines defined by iron railings, thousands of immigrants waited to be interrogated and examined. Inspectors asked them a list of questions ("Where did you come from?" "Where are you going?" "Do you have a job waiting for you?").

Doctors checked the newcomers' physical and mental health. They especially looked for any signs of contagious diseases. Those who didn't pass the health tests were sometimes **quarantined** for weeks in grim dormitories. The least fortunate were **deported** and sent back to their homelands.

At its peak in 1907, Ellis Island processed 5,000 people a day. In 1943, the receiving station was moved to Manhattan, but Ellis Island continued to be used as a detention center until it closed for good in November 1954.

About 40 percent of all Americans are descended from immigrants who came through Ellis Island.

Today, Ellis Island is part of the Statue of Liberty National Monument and houses a museum dedicated to the 12 million immigrants who passed through its doors.

A New York City health inspector examines newly arrived immigrant children in 1911.

The title of Jacob Riis's landmark book comes from the popular phrase "One half of the world does not know how the other half lives."

CHAPTER 17

TENEMENT LIFE

Life for new immigrants was grim,
but crusading journalists
worked to make it better.

MANY OF THE IMMIGRANTS WHO CAME through Ellis Island made their homes right where they landed, in New York City. Others traveled to cities such as Chicago, Boston, Philadelphia, Baltimore, and Washington, D.C. Wherever they went, they lived in similar squalor. Large families often squeezed together in small, cheaply made apartments called **tenements**. Jobs were scarce for the newcomers, but in time, many people found jobs in factories. Women typically worked in garment factories called **sweatshops**. Many of these workplaces were hot, crowded, and unsafe.

These downtrodden people found a champion in **Jacob Riis**. A journalist in New York City, Riis was himself an immigrant who had come to America at age 21 from Denmark. He prowled the city streets, interviewing and photographing immigrants. Riis collected his articles and photographs into a groundbreaking book titled *How the Other Half Lives*, published in 1890. The book shocked the public.

This photograph of a family in a New York tenement was taken by Lewis Hine, who was famous for taking photos of poor immigrants' homes and workplaces.

Although they often lived in small apartments, many immigrant families were very large.

CHAPTER 18

IMMIGRANT CHILDREN

While families arrived in America with a
common bond, they often became divided as
children assimilated and parents did not.

The typewriter was a recent invention during the Great Immigration!

I MMIGRANTS OFTEN CAME TO AMERICA TO MAKE a better life for their children. In American schools, children learned English and studied American history and culture. Nurses checked them for disease and taught them good **hygiene** and grooming. Children who didn't excel in academics had the opportunity to attend trade schools. Boys learned to be carpenters, sign painters, or janitors. Girls learned sewing, cooking, or typing.

But many children didn't get to finish elementary school—they had to go to work to help support their families. Working as unskilled laborers in factories and sweatshops, these young people were often exposed to unsafe and dangerous conditions. Laws against child labor came about because of this.

As immigrant children became assimilated into American society, many of their parents clung to the old ways and frequently didn't learn English. This often caused their children to look on them with embarrassment. But the children's skills were an asset to their parents. In many households, children took on adult roles, speaking in English to outsiders for their parents.

Children in Indiana work a night shift at a glass factory.

Foreign-language newspapers,
are a common sight in diverse
cities such as New York.

CHAPTER 19

ENRICHING THE LANGUAGE

Foreign-speaking immigrants brought their
languages with them, and some of their
words have rubbed off on English.

IMMIGRATION IS A TWO-WAY STREET. AS immigrants learned about America, America absorbed some of the immigrants' ways. Nowhere is this more apparent than in language. Hundreds of foreign words brought by immigrants have been adopted into everyday English.

If you've ever bought lunch at a "delicatessen," you've spoken German. If you've ordered "spaghetti" or "pizza," you've spoken Italian. If you've ever called someone a "klutz" (a clumsy person) or said they had "chutzpah" (nerve), you've spoken Yiddish, the language of many Jewish immigrants. If you've ever slept on a "cot," you've spoken Hindi, one of India's primary languages. If you've ever played a "banjo," you've spoken Bantu, an African language.

And then there are the hundreds of geographic places in the United States whose names are taken from the language of the immigrants who first settled there. These include states such as New Jersey (English) and California (Spanish) and cities such as Bismarck, North Dakota (German) and Odessa, Texas (Russian).

Odessa was named by Russian railroad workers who said the place reminded them of home.

These street signs in the International District neighborhood of Seattle, Washington, are written in both English and Chinese.

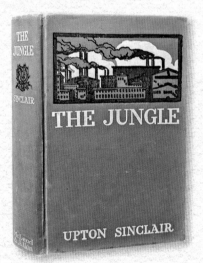

Upton Sinclair's 1906 novel The Jungle *helped lead to new laws regulating the meatpacking industry.*

CHAPTER 20

IMMIGRANTS IN LITERATURE

What Jacob Riis did for the immigrant experience in nonfiction, other writers did in stories and novels.

Sinclair's exposé was so convincing that it led to the passing of the first Pure Food and Drug Act by Congress.

AS IMMIGRANTS FLOODED AMERICA'S shores, writers told their stories in fiction. In *The Jungle* (1906), **Upton Sinclair** wrote about the trials and tragedies of a Lithuanian immigrant in Chicago. The book is also a graphic **exposé** of the terrible, unsanitary working conditions in the <u>meatpacking industry</u>.

Willa Cather's *My Antonia* (1918) dealt with an immigrant family from Bohemia (today's Czech Republic) living in Nebraska in the late 1800s. A second-generation Irish-American girl was the main character in Betty Smith's novel *A Tree Grows in Brooklyn* (1943). In his memoir *Angela's Ashes* (1996), American-born Frank McCourt wrote about his own family of Irish immigrants.

Mexican-American Sandra Cisneros drew on her own life growing up in Chicago for *The House on Mango Street* (1984), a blend of autobiography, poetry, and fiction. More recently, Afghan-American Khaled Hosseini wrote about an Afghan boy who flees war and terrorism in Kabul, Afghanistan, for a new life in the United States in *The Kite Runner* (2003). New generations of immigrant writers continue to bring the immigrant experience to life for readers.

Angela's Ashes was made into a popular film in 1999.

66 *[They are] beaten men from beaten races; representing the worst failures in the struggle for existence.* **99**

—MASSACHUSETTS INSTITUTE OF TECHNOLOGY
PRESIDENT FRANCIS A. WALKER,
WRITING OF IMMIGRANTS IN 1896

CHAPTER 21

WAR REFUGEES

The Great Immigration led to a backlash
against immigrants, but a world war
made them welcome again.

T HE MILLIONS OF IMMIGRANTS WHO CAME to America during the Great Immigration eventually led some Americans to resent and fear the newcomers. Congress responded by passing the Johnson-Reed Act in 1924, setting a limit of 150,000 immigrants from outside the Western Hemisphere each year. This total number was broken down into **quotas** nation by nation. During the Great Depression (1929–1939), more restrictions were placed on immigration so millions of unemployed Americans wouldn't have to compete with newcomers for jobs. These quotas affected persecuted groups in Europe, especially Jews in the late 1930s fleeing Nazi Germany, where millions were killed in the Holocaust.

The situation changed dramatically after World War II (1939–1945). The war left millions of Europeans homeless and poverty stricken. To assist them, Congress passed the Displaced Persons Act in 1948. The law allowed 205,000 war refugees into the United States. But a new war was brewing in Europe: the Cold War between the West and the **communist** Soviet Union. People looking to flee communism were welcomed to America.

By the time the act expired after several renewals in 1952, more than 415,000 displaced people from Europe had come to America.

European Jewish refugees during World War II line up at a U.S. Army base to receive soap and towels.

66 *I will support and defend the Constitution and the laws of the United States of America against all enemies . . .* **99**

—EXCERPT FROM THE OATH OF ALLEGIANCE FOR NEW CITIZENS

CHAPTER 22

THE ROAD TO CITIZENSHIP

The road to citizenship is not an easy one,
and things that natural-born Americans
take for granted are awarded to immigrants
only after a great deal of hard work.

To see if you could pass a citizenship test, go to page 132.

MANY IMMIGRANTS WANT TO BECOME American citizens. The process of naturalization had existed since 1790, but in 1952 it was detailed more clearly in the Immigration and Naturalization Act. Individuals wanting to become citizens have to meet a number of requirements. They have to be at least 18 years old. They also have to be able to read, write, and speak English and understand basic facts of American history and the American system of government. To become educated, many immigrants attend classes on English as a Second Language (ESL) and on American history and civics. They then have to pass a test on each of these topics.

Once they meet all these requirements, the applicants send their petitions and other documents to be examined by the U.S. Citizenship and Immigration Services (USCIS). About a month later, approved applicants attend a final hearing presided over by a federal judge, who administers the Oath of Allegiance. The immigrants leave the courtroom as full-fledged American citizens with the right to vote.

Naturalized citizens cannot serve as president or vice president, but have all other rights.

New U.S. citizens recite the Pledge of Allegiance during a naturalization ceremony in San Diego, California. Hundreds of thousand of people are naturalized each year.

*The first wave of Cuban
immigrants fleeing Castro's Cuba
arrive in the United States.*

OCT NOV DEC **1959** JAN FEB MAR

CHAPTER 23

THE CUBAN EXODUS

A 1959 revolution rocked the island nation of Cuba
and brought a new wave of immigrants to America.

As of the 2010 **census**, about 1.8 million Cuban Americans lived in the United States.

ON JANUARY 1, 1959, A REVOLUTION IN CUBA succeeded. Dictator Fulgencio Batista fled the country, and rebel leader Fidel Castro replaced Batista's dictatorship with a communist government. Castro seized the property and businesses of many Cubans. Thousands fled their homeland for the United States with nothing but the clothes on their backs. The U.S. government <u>welcomed the refugees</u> under a special **humanitarian** provision. In 1980, Castro allowed many other people to leave the country by boat for the United States. These Cuban exiles were also welcomed.

Most of the new Cuban immigrants settled in Florida. Today, Miami, the state's largest city, is 70 percent Latino, and 54 percent of these Latinos are Cuban. They play a major role in the city's government, social life, and culture. In December 2014, U.S. **president Barack Obama** and Cuban president Raul Castro normalized relations between their two countries for the first time in decades. However, in 2017, **President Donald Trump** announced that he would pull back Obama's attempts to improve America's relationship with Cuba.

A raft filled with Cuban refugees makes its way toward Florida.

Helicopters like this one were used to help people escape from Vietnam at the end of the Vietnam War.

CHAPTER 24

REFUGEES FROM VIETNAM

War divided the Vietnamese people, but many of the defeated have found a new home in the United States.

FROM 1955 TO 1975, VIETNAM WAS SPLIT in two during a civil war between the communist government in the North and the U.S.-supported South. April 30, 1975, was an unforgettable day for South Vietnam. North Vietnamese forces stormed Saigon, the capital city of South Vietnam. Thousands of South Vietnamese rushed to the U.S. embassy, where Americans were being evacuated by helicopter. Some of the South Vietnamese were taken to America, but millions were left behind, where many were imprisoned in "reeducation camps" run by Vietnam's communist government. However, they were not forgotten. Later that year, many more South Vietnamese were welcomed to the United States. These first Vietnamese immigrants after the war were military or government personnel or other well-educated professionals.

A few years later, greater numbers of South Vietnamese fled Vietnam for the United States by water and came to be known as the "boat people." They were mostly from rural areas and were less educated. By 2014, there were 1.3 million Vietnamese immigrants living in the United States.

Nearly 40 percent of all Vietnamese immigrants live in California. There are also large numbers of Vietnamese in Texas, Washington State, and Florida.

Evacuees load onto a helicopter near the U.S. embassy in Vietnam at the end of the war in April 1975.

" *I am a New York, Brooklyn, Jewish guy who just happened to be born in Moscow.* **"**

—COMEDIAN OLEG BOKSNER

CHAPTER 25

LAUGHING AT EACH OTHER: IMMIGRANT HUMOR

Humor shows how immigrant groups are
unique, but it also shows how their experiences
as immigrants are not so different.

ETHNIC HUMOR HAS BEEN A FORM OF entertainment in America since the Great Immigration. Today, immigrants and the children of immigrants are sharing the humor of the immigrant experience with American audiences on television and in movies. New York City, a melting pot of multiculturalism, has a lively comedy club scene that includes many immigrant comics. At some venues, comedians perform in their own languages for people from their home countries.

Immigrant cartoonists have also weighed in on immigrant issues. Colombian-born cartoonist and children's book illustrator Juana Medina created the comic, "I Juana Live in America." It describes with both humor and seriousness her 10-year ordeal to get a visa to join her parents in Washington, D.C. As Russian-Jewish comedian Oleg Boksner puts it, there is something universal in the specifics of each immigrant's journey: "I've had people from Mexico relate to [my jokes] as well, because they relate to the difficulties of being an immigrant in one form or another."

Early comedians such as the team of Edward Harrigan and Tony Hart, who played Irish characters in their songs and skits, were often not immigrants themselves.

A sign warns drivers to watch out for people who have crossed the border from Mexico to the United States.

CHAPTER 26

FLEEING TO EL NORTE

Cubans are not the only refugees from Latin America
seeking a better life in the United States.

BEGINNING IN THE 1960S, <u>THOUSANDS</u> <u>of immigrants from Mexico, Central America, and the Caribbean</u> islands began pouring into the United States. They were fleeing poverty, crime, and civil war. Mexico, which is one of the top origins of immigrants to the United States, has major troubles with crime and violence and a lack of good jobs. Honduras remains one of the murder capitals of the world. Haiti is the poorest country in the Western Hemisphere.

Forced to emigrate to survive, many of these mostly Hispanic newcomers headed north through Mexico to <u>"El Norte"</u> (the North). Desperate for a better life, many of these refugees cross the border illegally to get into the United States. They face deadly desert conditions, untrustworthy guides who charge high prices for transporting them, and the danger of arrest by American authorities and deportation back to their homeland. Many die along the way.

El Norte is Spanish for "the north."

A group of young men attempt to enter the United States illegally by climbing a fence along the border between Mexico and Arizona.

Tacos, a favorite food for many
Americans, were brought to the United
States by Mexican immigrants.

CHAPTER 27

NEW FOODS FROM THE OLD COUNTRY

The foods of immigrants have worked their way into American homes, hearts, and stomachs.

FAMILIAR FOODS ARE A UNIVERSAL SOURCE of comfort, especially for immigrants. By cooking the foods their parents and grandparents made, newcomers feel less lonely in a strange, new land. In a way, they've carried a little piece of the old country with them. At first, many of these ethnic dishes were served primarily in the home or at family gatherings and celebrations. But over time, they were being eaten by other Americans in restaurants, many of them run and owned by immigrants.

Chinese immigrants operate restaurants that have introduced Cantonese and spicy Szechuan specialties to American patrons. The Germans brought over frankfurters (hot dogs) smothered in sauerkraut. Pierogies are Polish dumplings filled with meat, potatoes, fruit, or other ingredients. Borscht is a Russian beet soup. Italians introduced America to a bewildering <u>variety of pastas</u>, from vermicelli and linguine to lasagna and ravioli. Mexican immigrants brought such foods as tacos, tortillas, and salsa. If America, as some people say, is a melting pot of many immigrants, that pot is filled with a rich range of delicious foods.

Italian pizza was not popular in the United States until American soldiers brought it back with them from Italy after World War II (1939–1945).

Cooks prepare food at a restaurant in San Francisco's Chinatown.

Some immigrants, such as former governor of California Arnold Schwarzenegger, have become important American leaders.

CHAPTER 28

IMMIGRANTS WHO MADE GOOD

There are many success stories among immigrants—some have even become famous.

I N THE 1930S, EUROPE SUFFERED UNDER repressive governments, prompting some of its best and brightest to emigrate to America. The stream of talent included German Jewish physicist Albert Einstein and Italian scientist Enrico Fermi, who was a key figure in the development of the atomic bomb.

Later generations of immigrants have continued to make good in America. Austrian Arnold Schwarzenegger went from being a famed bodybuilder to being an even more famous action hero in movies and then governor of California. Indian American M. Night Shyamalan is the director of such films as *The Sixth Sense* and *Split*. Chinese immigrant David Ho is a pioneering researcher in the fight against AIDS. Actor Will Arnett, whose films include *Ratatouille* and *The Lego Movie*, is a Canadian immigrant. Without the contributions of these and many other famous immigrants, the country would be a poorer place.

Physicist Albert Einstein was in the United States at the time the Nazis took control of his native Germany. Because he was Jewish, Einstein chose to stay and become a U.S. citizen rather than face the dangers of returning home.

**"** We've lost control of our own borders, and no nation can do that and survive.**"**

—President Ronald Reagan, 1984

CHAPTER 29

ILLEGAL IMMIGRATION

Illegal immigration is a problem the United States
has been grappling with for a long time.

THERE ARE MORE THAN 11 MILLION undocumented immigrants in the United States today. Many of them crossed over the country's southern border from Mexico. A majority of undocumented immigrants are Latin. Only a quarter of them come from other countries such as China.

Immigrating to the United States legally can be difficult. Close relatives of U.S. citizens, such as spouses or parents, have an easier time getting approval. So do people with skills or jobs that are in high demand, such as doctors and engineers. For people who do not meet these qualifications, the process can take years or possibly never happen at all. As a result, many come to the United States illegally.

Illegal immigration is a difficult issue, and the government has long struggled to find a workable solution to it. Some Americans would like to make legal immigration easier, while others share the anti-immigrant feelings of past generations and want to stop illegal immigration and restrict legal entry into the United States.

A member of the U.S. Border Patrol looks toward Mexico from Arizona.

“My fellow Americans, we are and always will be a nation of immigrants. We were strangers once, too.”

—President Barack Obama, 2014

CHAPTER 30

IMMIGRATION TODAY

The debate over immigration in our
complicated world continues.

AMERICA IS A NATION OF IMMIGRANTS. Everyone's ancestors came to the country from someplace else. From its beginnings as a nation, the United States has been home to people from everywhere around the globe. But in the 21st century, many Americans are questioning the country's commitment to letting newcomers in. Many people feel that immigrants are taking jobs away from American citizens. They also think immigrants are crowding schools and hospitals. However, most economists believe that immigration is good for the economy. President Donald Trump wants to drastically increase restrictions on immigration. Other Americans believe the process by which immigrants are allowed into the United States is already strict enough.

Immigrants throughout U.S. history have benefited greatly from living in America, and America in turn has benefited from immigrants' energy and skills. Can America continue to be a nation of immigrants? There is no easy answer, but it is a question we have to keep probing.

Americans can trace their roots back to every other country in the world.

MAPS

TOP REGION OF BIRTH BY STATE, 2009–2013

Immigrants come to the United States from all around the world. This map shows which region of the world most immigrants come from in each U.S. state.

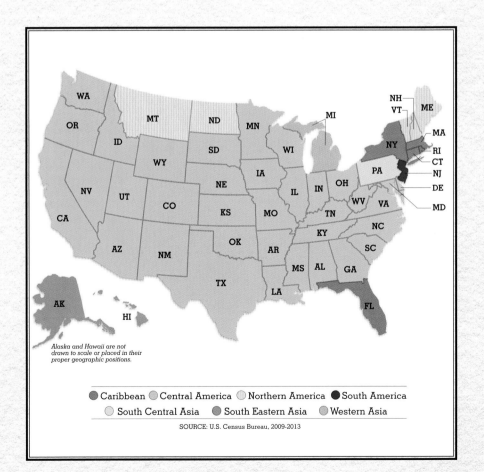

Alaska and Hawaii are not drawn to scale or placed in their proper geographic positions.

● Caribbean ○ Central America ○ Northern America ● South America
○ South Central Asia ● South Eastern Asia ○ Western Asia

SOURCE: U.S. Census Bureau, 2009-2013

TOP COUNTRIES OF ORIGIN FOR LEGAL IMMIGRANTS IN THE UNITED STATES, 2013–2015.

Legal immigrants only make up a part of the total number of immigrants to the United States each year. Many people cross the country's borders illegally. This makes it difficult for the government to keep track of certain immigration statistics.

This chart shows the top countries that the United States' legal immigrants came from between 2013 and 2015.

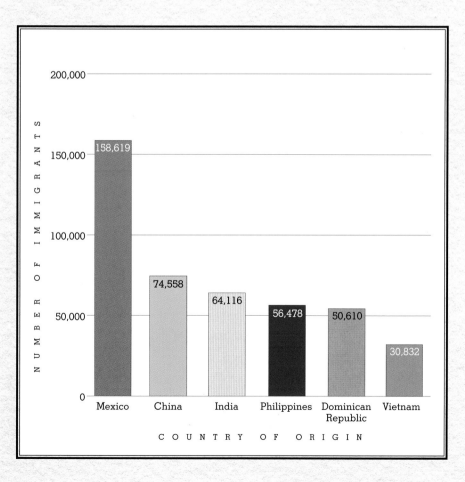

COULD YOU PASS THE U.S. CITIZENSHIP TEST?

QUESTIONS

Here are 10 questions you might have to answer if you were taking the U.S. citizenship test. New citizens must be able to answer at least six of the questions correctly. Can you pass?

1. What do we call the first 10 amendments to the Constitution?

2. How many U.S. senators are there?

3. How old do citizens have to be to vote for president?

4. Who was president during the Great Depression and World War II?

5. Name one state that borders Mexico.

6. Who is the "father of our country"?

7. When was the Declaration of Independence adopted?

8. Who is in charge of the executive branch?

9. What movement tried to end racial discrimination?

10. What ocean is on the west coast of the United States?

ANSWERS

1. The Bill of Rights; 2. 100; 3. 18 or older; 4. Franklin D. Roosevelt; 5. California, Arizona, New Mexico, or Texas; 6. George Washington; 7. 1776; 8. The president; 9. The civil rights movement; 10. The Pacific Ocean

KEY PLAYERS

Father Junipero Serra has been called the "apostle of California" for helping to establish 21 Spanish missions there in the 1700s. Although he was known as a strong defender of the Native Americans who lived and worked at the missions, historians have more recently accused him of mistreating them.

President Millard Fillmore (1850–1853) served as the 13th president of the United States. He also ran for president in 1856 on the ticket of the anti-immigration American Party, known as the Know-Nothing Party, but won only one state.

Frederic Auguste Bartholdi was a French sculptor who created the Statue of Liberty, which he called *Liberty Enlightening the World*. The French people gave the statue to America as a gift, and for many years it served as a welcoming symbol to millions of immigrants as they entered New York Harbor.

Emma Lazarus was a poet and social activist from New York City. She wrote "The New Colossus," the poem inscribed in the pedestal of the Statue of Liberty.

Jacob Riis was a crusading journalist and reformer who exposed the terrible living and working conditions of immigrants in New York City in the late 1800s and early 1900s.

Upton Sinclair wrote about the difficulties of immigrant life in his novel *The Jungle*. The book also exposed the poor conditions in America's meatpacking industry.

President Barack Obama (2009–2016) was the first African American U.S. president. Among his achievements as president include the Affordable Care Act, which is widely known as Obamacare, and the reopening of relations with Cuba.

President Donald Trump (2017–) ran on a platform that called for stricter regulations on legal immigration and a harder line on illegal immigration, including the building of a wall along the U.S.-Mexico border.

IMMIGRATION TIMELINE

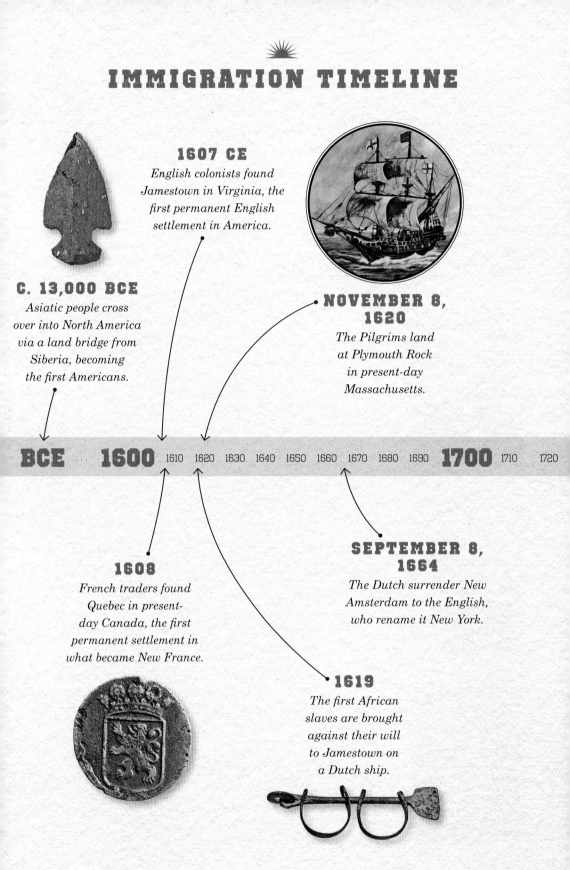

1607 CE
English colonists found Jamestown in Virginia, the first permanent English settlement in America.

C. 13,000 BCE
Asiatic people cross over into North America via a land bridge from Siberia, becoming the first Americans.

NOVEMBER 8, 1620
The Pilgrims land at Plymouth Rock in present-day Massachusetts.

BCE ... 1600 · 1610 · 1620 · 1630 · 1640 · 1650 · 1660 · 1670 · 1680 · 1690 · 1700 · 1710 · 1720

1608
French traders found Quebec in present-day Canada, the first permanent settlement in what became New France.

SEPTEMBER 8, 1664
The Dutch surrender New Amsterdam to the English, who rename it New York.

1619
The first African slaves are brought against their will to Jamestown on a Dutch ship.

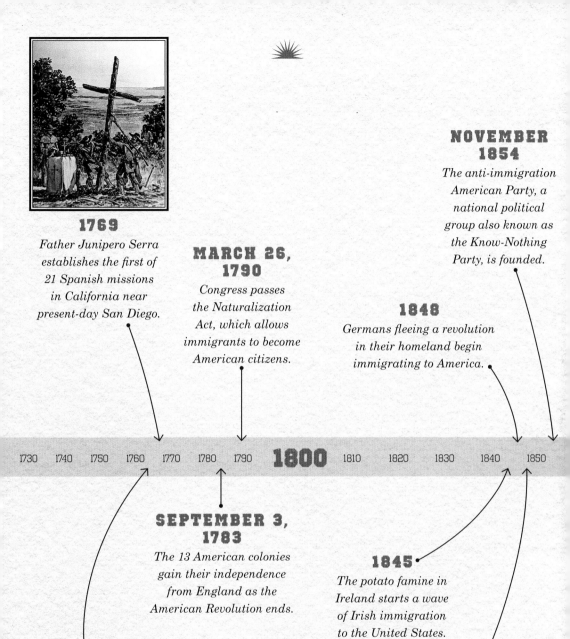

1769

Father Junipero Serra establishes the first of 21 Spanish missions in California near present-day San Diego.

MARCH 26, 1790

Congress passes the Naturalization Act, which allows immigrants to become American citizens.

NOVEMBER 1854

The anti-immigration American Party, a national political group also known as the Know-Nothing Party, is founded.

1848

Germans fleeing a revolution in their homeland begin immigrating to America.

| 1730 | 1740 | 1750 | 1760 | 1770 | 1780 | 1790 | **1800** | 1810 | 1820 | 1830 | 1840 | 1850 |

SEPTEMBER 3, 1783

The 13 American colonies gain their independence from England as the American Revolution ends.

1845

The potato famine in Ireland starts a wave of Irish immigration to the United States.

1763

The English defeat the French in North America in the French and Indian War.

APRIL 1849

Chinese immigrants begin to arrive in California, following the discovery of gold there the previous year.

MAY 6, 1882

Congress passes the
Chinese Exclusion Act,
ending immigration
from China for the
next 61 years.

1906

Upton Sinclair's novel
The Jungle, *an exposé
of the meatpacking
industry where
many immigrants
work, is published.*

MAY 10, 1869

The first
transcontinental
railroad is completed
in Utah, having been
largely built by Chinese
and Irish immigrants.

1890

Journalist Jacob Riis
publishes his exposé
of urban immigrant
life, How the Other
Half Lives.

| 1860 | 1870 | 1880 | 1890 | **1900** | 1910 |

1880–1920

The Great Immigration
is under way, bringing
millions of immigrants
to America from
Scandinavia and eastern
and southern Europe.

JANUARY 1, 1892

The receiving station for
new immigrants officially
opens on Ellis Island
in New York Harbor.

OCTOBER 28, 1886

The Statue of Liberty,
a gift from France,
is dedicated in New
York Harbor.

JUNE 25, 1948

The Displaced Persons Act goes into effect, allowing hundreds of thousands of World War II refugees to enter the United States.

NOVEMBER 9, 2016

Donald Trump is elected president after advocating stricter enforcement of immigration policies and the building of a wall on the U.S.-Mexico border to prevent people from illegally entering the United States.

1959

The first refugees from Fidel Castro's Cuba arrive in America.

| 1920 | 1930 | 1940 | 1950 | 1960 | 1970 | 1980 | 1990 | **2000** | 2010 | 2020 |

MAY 26, 1924

Congress passes the Johnson-Reed Act, strictly limiting the number of immigrants allowed into the United States from each country.

1975

Following the end of the Vietnam War, the first South Vietnamese refugees come to the United States.

JANUARY 27, 2017

President Trump issues an executive order to temporarily ban people from seven primarily Muslim countries from entering the United States.

JUNE 27, 1952

Congress passes the Immigration and Naturalization Act, codifying the requirements for citizenship.

GLOSSARY

- **assimilated** (uh-SIM-uh-lay-tid) *verb* became part of the culture of where you're living by becoming more like it

- **blight** (BLITE) *noun* a disease that kills plants

- **census** (SEN-suhs) *noun* the official count of a country's population

- **communist** (KAHM-yuh-nist) *adjective* relating to an economic system in which all the land, property, businesses, and resources belong to the government or community, not individuals

- **democracy** (duh-MAH-kruh-see) *noun* a style of government in which people choose leaders by voting in elections

- **deported** (dih-POR-tid) *verb* expelled from a country

- **emigrated** (EM-uh-gray-tid) *verb* moved from one country to settle in another country

- **exposé** (ek-spoh-ZAY) *noun* the public disclosure of something secret or disreputable

- **humanitarian** (hyoo-man-uh-TARE-ee-uhn) *adjective* concerned with the general welfare of humanity

- **hygiene** (HYE-jeen) *noun* practices leading to good health

- **indentured servants** (in-DEN-churd SUR-vuhnts) *noun* persons bound by contract to serve another person for a set period of time

- **missions** (MISH-uhnz) *noun* places where religious leaders help, educate, and train groups of converts

- **naturalized** (NATCH-ur-uh-lyzd) *verb* accepted as an official citizen of a country

- **pogroms** (puh-GRAHMZ) *noun* the organized persecution and killing of Jews in Russia and eastern Europe during the late 19th century

- **quarantined** (KWOR-uhn-teend) *verb* isolated people to prevent the spread of a disease

- **quotas** (KWOH-tuhz) *noun* fixed numbers or proportions of certain groups of people

- **steerage** (STEER-ij) *noun* the lower part of a passenger ship where passengers paying the cheapest fares stayed

- **sweatshops** (SWET-shahps) *noun* businesses where workers are taken advantage of by being forced to work long hours for low wages, often in poor or unsafe conditions

- **tenements** (TEN-uh-muhnts) *noun* apartment buildings that are poorly built and maintained

FIND OUT MORE

BOOKS

Baker, Bryon. *U.S. Immigration in the 1900s.* North Mankato, MN: Capstone Press, 2015.

Demuth, Patricia Brenna. *What Was Ellis Island?* New York: Grosset & Dunlap, 2014.

FILMS

America America (1963). DVD, Warner Bros., 2011.

El Norte (1983). DVD, Criterion Collection, 2009.

The Emigrants/The New Land (1971/72). DVD box set, Criterion Collection, 2016.

In America (2002). DVD, Fox Searchlight, 2004.

NOTE: *Some books and films may not be appropriate for younger viewers.*

VISIT THIS SCHOLASTIC WEBSITE FOR MORE INFORMATION ABOUT **IMMIGRATION**

www.factsfornow.scholastic.com

Enter the keywords **IMMIGRATION**

INDEX

ABOUT THE AUTHOR

Steven Otfinoski has written more than 190 books for young readers. Three of his books have been named to the New York Public Library's list of recommendations, Books for the Teen Age. He also teaches college English and creative writing. He lives with his wife in Connecticut.